T0328574

Cambridge Elements ≡

Elements in Public Economics
edited by
Robin Boadway
Queen's University
Frank A. Cowell
London School of Economics and Political Science
Massimo Florio
University of Milan

THE ECONOMICS OF SOCIAL PROTECTION

Pierre Pestieau
*HEC, University of Liège and CORE,
University of Louvain*

CAMBRIDGE
UNIVERSITY PRESS

Shaftesbury Road, Cambridge CB2 8EA, United Kingdom

One Liberty Plaza, 20th Floor, New York, NY 10006, USA

477 Williamstown Road, Port Melbourne, VIC 3207, Australia

314–321, 3rd Floor, Plot 3, Splendor Forum, Jasola District Centre, New Delhi – 110025, India

103 Penang Road, #05–06/07, Visioncrest Commercial, Singapore 238467

Cambridge University Press is part of Cambridge University Press & Assessment, a department of the University of Cambridge.

We share the University's mission to contribute to society through the pursuit of education, learning and research at the highest international levels of excellence.

www.cambridge.org
Information on this title: www.cambridge.org/9781009295482
DOI: 10.1017/9781009295475

© Pierre Pestieau 2023

This publication is in copyright. Subject to statutory exception and to the provisions of relevant collective licensing agreements, no reproduction of any part may take place without the written permission of Cambridge University Press & Assessment.

First published 2023

A catalogue record for this publication is available from the British Library.

ISBN 978-1-009-45415-5 Hardback
ISBN 978-1-009-29548-2 Paperback
ISSN 2516-2276 (online)
ISSN 2516-2268 (print)

Cambridge University Press & Assessment has no responsibility for the persistence or accuracy of URLs for external or third-party internet websites referred to in this publication and does not guarantee that any content on such websites is, or will remain, accurate or appropriate.

The Economics of Social Protection

Elements in Public Economics

DOI: 10.1017/9781009295475
First published online: August 2023

Pierre Pestieau
HEC, University of Liège and CORE, University of Louvain

Author for correspondence: Pierre Pestieau, p.pestieau@ulg.ac.be

Abstract: The objective of this Element is to provide an analysis of social protection from an economic perspective. It relies on tools and methods widely used in public and insurance economics and comprises four main sections besides the introduction. The first section is devoted to the design of social protection programs and their political sustainability. The second section assesses the efficiency and performance of social protection programs, and of the welfare state as a whole. In the third section, the relative merits of social and private insurance are analyzed as well as the design of optimum insurance contracts with emphasis on health and pensions. The last section focuses on the implications of asymmetric information that may lead governments to adopt policies that would otherwise be rejected in a perfect information setting.

Keywords: welfare state, social protection, private and social insurance, social assistance, redistribution

ISBNs: 9781009454155 (HB), 9781009295482 (PB), 9781009295475 (OC)
ISSNs: 2516-2276 (online), 2516-2268 (print)

Contents

1 Introduction

In this introductory part, we present the basic concepts and some evidence concerning social protection. In particular we define the welfare state, social protection, and social insurance. We also introduce some taxonomies of the welfare state, the most important being based on the redistributive nature and the size of the programs.

1.1 Definition

It is not easy to give a good definition of either the welfare state or social protection.[1] To paraphrase Anthony Atkinson (1991), there is indeed a lot of the proverbial elephant in the room as regards social protection and the welfare state: we may not be able to define this elephant, but we can recognize one when we see it. The usual way is to list the objectives to be pursued and the instruments used to achieve them. Accordingly, social protection is composed of a set of actions financed by the state that (i) support individuals and families in dealing with vulnerabilities during their lifecycle, (ii) help especially the poor and vulnerable groups in having the resilience to respond to crisis and shocks, including social-environmental risks, and (iii) favor social inclusion and support families. More specifically, social protection helps in coping with the various lifetime risks linked to unemployment, disability, sickness, early or late death, retirement, and family. And it strives to alleviate both temporary and permanent poverty and income inequality. The standard instruments are transfers or the provision of services such as education and housing. Both health and long-term care can be directly provided by the state or indirectly through transfers that allow one to pay for those services. Among the transfers, one can distinguish between those of social assistance, generally based on means-testing, and those of social insurance that are in great part contributory. Figure 1 provides a sketch of the main components of the welfare state and of social protection. One sees that the welfare state comprises social protection but also benefits in kind such as education and social housing. From this figure, one sees the distinction made between the welfare state and social protection.

This taxonomy can be discussed. For example, family allowances can be part of social insurance as they are in most European countries, or they can be attached to social assistance. In this Element, benefits in kind are only dealt with in Section 5.3. Furthermore, the objectives mentioned earlier can be achieved not only with budgetary means but also with a number of nonbudgetary tools. Among them are the laws; for example, the law that constrains builders to

---

[1] For a good overview, see Barr (2020) and Pestieau and Lefebvre (2018).

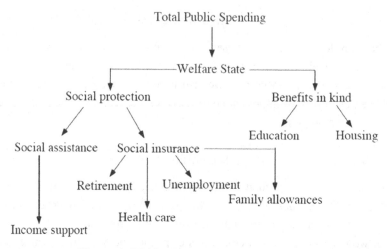

Figure 1 Welfare state and social protection

include in their constructions amenities that are friendly to handicapped people or the law that forces employers to hire a certain number of handicapped workers. There is also the legislation protecting workers against on-the-job accidents. Furthermore, there are several private social protection arrangements that, although mandatory, are not financed through funds that are part of public spending. These include mandatory private pensions and health care insurance. The importance and generosity[2] of the welfare state are usually measured by the share of social spending in GDP. This share has a rather wide range across industrialized countries, from 13.4 percent in Ireland to 31 percent in France for the year 2019. Note, however, that if we take into account mandatory private protection spending and the taxation of social benefits to obtain what is called the generosity of net social spending, this range narrows. For example, whereas the share of gross social spending in 2017 was equal to 18.4 percent in the United States versus 31.5 percent in France, in net terms, it was 31.1 percent in France and 29.7 percent in the United States.[3]

1.2 The Crisis of the Welfare State

Even though the generosity of the welfare state has been increasing almost everywhere and converging across countries, a number of books and plenty of articles and reports have been written over the last decades to indicate that the welfare state is in crisis. There is some discontent that reaches a peak with the emergence of populist movements and the various social divides that have

---

[2] Throughout this Element, generosity means the level of social benefits.
[3] Adema (2001), Adema et al. (2011).

emerged lately. One major critique is that the welfare state may have focused too much on poverty alleviation and inequality reduction and not enough on social mobility. Plenty of evidence shows that the social elevator does not work anymore, and this generates frustration among people who don't see any prospects for them and their children.[4] A related criticism is that the welfare state is ill-adapted to current problems. This is because it was designed several decades ago in a world where there was little mobility of factors and the ensuing social dumping, the labor market was less precarious, family solidarity was stronger, and there was more compliance. Demographic aging is also making things difficult. Given these assessments, there is a clear need to design social policy that meets those new challenges.

1.3 Types of Welfare State

There does not exist a single model of welfare state in the OECD countries. Each country has its own model that is the result of its political and social culture and of its economic evolution. There exists a number of taxonomies of welfare states which focus on specific features of their functioning. Economists tend to focus on a taxonomy based on two characteristics: the generosity and the redistributiveness of programs. The main interest of distinguishing among types of social protection programs is the different implications they have in terms of efficiency, equity, and political sustainability. To measure the redistributiveness, one can use the progressivity index I_R that for each program looks at $I_R = 1 - G(b)/G(w)$ where $G(b)$ is the Gini of benefits and $G(w)$ is the Gini of income.[5] If the program is contributory, that is, the benefits are closely linked to income or contributions, $I_R = 0$. If, on the contrary, the benefits are flat, unrelated to contributions, then $I_R = 1$. Using those two characteristics, generosity and redistributiveness, one can distinguish among three main types of welfare states:

- Those which are redistributive and generous. Typically, the Nordic countries.
- Those which are contributory and generous. They are also called Bismarckian and comprise Germany, France, and Italy.
- Those which are redistributive but not generous. These are labeled Beveridgean and are the Anglo-Saxon countries.

---

[4] OECD (2018).
[5] Biggs et al. (2009).

In Section 2, we come back to the distinction between Bismarckian and Beveridgean programs, named after two famous founders of social protection, Otto von Bismarck and William Beveridge.

Sociologist Esping-Andersen (1990) used the concept of "decommodification" of social protection to rank countries. Decommodification means that services are rendered and transfers are made as a matter of right, without reliance on the market. Using a number of indicators, he rates his sample of welfare states according to their decommodification score. This allows him to distinguish among three welfare state regimes: the Anglo-Saxon "new" nations are all concentrated at the bottom of his index; the Scandinavian countries are at the top; in between, we find the continental European countries, some of which, like Belgium and the Netherlands, fall close to the Nordic cluster. Besides the preceding taxonomy, three related concepts are often used to distinguish among welfare states. These are activation, responsibility, and individualization. The first line of separation is the extent to which those benefiting from social benefits are induced to get out from the state of dependence in which they are. The Danish flexicurity program is typical of such a proactive option. Another line of separation is between countries where benefits are only awarded when benefiters are deemed unlucky and not responsible for what they are. Finally, there is the distinction between programs that focus on the individual and others that are targeted to the family unit. As will be seen, those distinctions can have important implications regarding the financial and political sustainability of social protection and they impact the standard trade-off between equity and efficiency.

2 Design and Sustainability

This section is devoted to the idea that a well-designed social protection should be both financially and politically sustainable. And we introduce the key trade-off between the redistributive nature of a program and its political support.

2.1 Bismarck versus Beveridge

The issue at hand is to choose either politically or normatively a type of social protection system that is politically sustainable. We choose the example of pensions, but the issue of political support applies as well to other parts of social protection. We consider a society consisting of N types of individuals i. An individual of type i is characterized by a labor productivity or wage, w_i. There are n_i individuals of type i. Each individual lives two periods. They work during the first period and retire in the second period. They allocate their earnings, net of a contribution to the pension system, between first-period consumption and saving. Second-period consumption is equal to the pension denoted p_i, plus the returns from saving. The pension system is here assumed to be fully funded, namely behaving like private saving. Individual i's lifetime utility is

$$U_i = u(c_i) + \beta u(d_i) = u(w_i(1 - \tau) - s_i) + \beta u((1 + r)s_i + p_i),$$

where

$$p_i = (1 + r)\tau (\alpha w_i + (1 - \alpha)\bar{w}).$$

We use the following notation:

- $u(.)$ is a strictly concave utility function;
- c and d are respectively first- and second-period consumption;
- s is saving;
- β is the time preference factor;
- τ is the payroll tax;
- w_i and r are respectively the wage level and the interest rate;
- $\bar{w} = \sum_{i=1}^{\bar{N}} n_i w_i$ is the average wage level.

Finally, the parameter α is the Bismarckian parameter that can be related to the progressivity index defined earlier. Instead of using the Gini coefficient, we can use the variance of either pension benefits or earnings. We thus have $I_R = 1 - V(p)/V(w) = 1 - \alpha^2\tau^2(1 + r)^2$, where $V(.)$ stands for variance. A pure Bismarckian system is such that pension contribution and saving bring the same return and are thus equivalent. A pure Beveridgean system is such that everyone gets the same pension irrespective of their contribution.

We now allow for some work in the second period. Let z be the fraction of second period devoted to work. Given that each period has a length of 1, the age of retirement is $1 + z$ and the length of life 2. We assume that the individual can choose z and that earnings in the second period are taxed. Finally, the disutility of postponing retirement is $v(z) = z^2/2$, a strictly convex function. We now write the lifetime utility of individual i as

$$U_i = u(w_i(1 - \tau) - s_i) + \beta u((1 + r)s_i + w_i(1 - \tau)z_i + p_i - z_i^2/2),$$

where

$$p_i = \tau \{\alpha [(1 + r)w_i + w_i z_i] + (1-\alpha) [(1 + r)\bar{w} + \overline{wz}]\}$$

and

$$\overline{wz} = \sum_i n_i w_i z_i.$$

Maximizing U_i with respect to s_i and z_i, we obtain the following FOCs (first-order conditions):

$$u'(c_i) = \beta(1 + r)u'(d_i)$$

and

$$z_i = w_i[1 - \tau(1 - \alpha)],$$

where we implictly assume that the choice of z_i does not affect $\overline{wz}$.

If $\beta(1 + r) = 1$, we have equality between the two consumption levels. When $\tau = 0$, $z_i = w_i$. We clearly see that with the Beveridgean regime, there is an incentive to retire earlier than with a contributory regime. In fact, when $\alpha = 1$, the pension system is neutral toward the retirement decision. We come back to this issue in Section 4.5.1.

2.2 Optimal Design

It is legitimate to look for the pension design that would maximize a utilitarian social welfare function such as

$$SW = \Sigma_i n_i v_i [u(c_i) + \beta u(d_i)],$$

where n_i is the relative number of type i's individuals and v_i is the social weight given to type i. Those social weights make it possible to encompass the case where the objective would be the Rawlsian maximin, namely the maximization of the utility of the worst-off. One easily checks that, without liquidity constraints (saving can be negative) and with fixed age of retirement (z is a constant), the solution would be $\alpha = 0; \tau = 1$. Otherwise, the problem gets more complicated and the solution depends on key factors:

- liquidity constraints ($s_i \geq 0$)
- tax distortions
- social weights
- the wage distribution.

With plausible assumptions, the solution is $\alpha \leq 0; 1 > \tau > 0$.

Note that $\alpha < 0$ amounts to a means-testing regime. The pension level decreases with the level of wage:

$$\frac{dp_i}{dw_i} = \tau\alpha [1 + r + z_i] < 0.$$

The implication of this result is that normally the optimal scheme implies means testing or at least a flat rate benefit. We illustrate this point with a simple example of an economy where the interest rate is nil, there is no time preference and no work in the second period. The individual's utility is

$$U_i = u(c_i) + u(d_i) = u(w_i(1 - \tau) - s_i) + u((s + \tau [\alpha w_i + (1 - \alpha)\bar{w}]).$$

In case there is no liquidity constraint, namely saving can be negative, we have that $c_i = d_i$ and thus

$$c_i = d_i = \frac{w_i - \tau (1 - \alpha)(w_i - \bar{w})}{2}.$$

It is clear that social welfare is maximized when $\tau = 1$ and $\alpha = 0$. With these parameters, we have

$$c_i = d_i = \bar{w}/2.$$

Note that if the tax rate is limited to a value below 1, the same result can be obtained by having a value of α below 0 such that $\tau (1 - \alpha) = 1$. The problem is that such an optimal scheme is not politically sustainable. As soon as introduced, it is subject to progressive erosion. The middle class that is needed to gather a majority in favor of the pension system does not find it attractive.

A combination of Beveridge and Bismarck is to be chosen. And in fact, this solution will even be preferable for the poor.

2.3 Political Support

The preceding optimal solution might end up lacking political support according to the idea that a program exclusively targeted to the poor tends to become a poor program. Lack of political majority leads to a slow erosion of such a program. To formalize this idea, we adopt a two-stage collective choice: first, the choice of α, and second, the choice of τ (majority voting). The choice of α could be normative or positive, in which case we would have sequential voting, first for α and then for τ.

In Casamatta et al. (2000), α is chosen according to the Rawlsian maximin criterion on the basis of a relation $\tau(\alpha)$ that is obtained from majority voting on τ, given the parameter α. With well-behaved utility functions, Casamatta et al. obtain a solution with both parameters between zero and one and a positive correlation between them. Empirically, this correlation can be verified.[6]

To make the point that a program for the poor is politically unsustainable, let us use a simple model wherein each individual pays a tax on their earnings

---

[6] Conde-Ruiz and Profeta (2007).

to finance a uniform benefit to the poor, namely those with income below w_P. The utility of each individual is given by

$$U_i = u(w_i(1 - \tau) + b_i),$$

where $b_i = \hat{b}$ for $i < P$ and $b_i = 0$ for $i \geq P$. The median income is w_m that is larger than w_P and smaller than $\overline{w} = \sum n_i w_i$.

If this benefit is chosen by majority voting, it is pretty clear that the median voter will vote against it. To support it, one should award all individuals the benefit $\hat{b} = \tau \overline{w}$. In that case the median voter will back it, given that they pay τw_m and obtain $\tau \overline{w}$.

To conclude, a more redistributive program calls for a more generous program. This has been called the paradox of redistribution (see Section 3.1).

2.4 Notional Accounts

Assume that we have a pension system with a given α. Some economists believe that instead of having a hybrid system, it would be preferable to split the system into two parts: a purely redistributive one providing a flat-rate pension and a purely Bismarckian one that would be purely contributive and mimic a private scheme. Their concern is that when making decisions within the hybrid system, individuals consider that their tax is fully distortive. In other words, their perceived α, denoted α^P, is equal to zero and thus, in the preceding example, they retire at $z = w(1 - \tau)$ and not at $z = w(1 - \tau(1 - \alpha))$. On the contrary, some other economists, close to labor unions, are in favor of the hybrid system, convinced that the perceived α is equal to one and thus that $z = w$. In their view, the pension system is a social compact, a common good, that brings utility to everyone.

The same reasoning applies to the whole social protection. In many countries, about two-thirds of social spending concerns lifetime redistribution.[7] This includes branches such as health, education, pension, long-term care, and unemployment. For these branches, one could have individual notional accounts that would start at birth and end at death and that would be actuarially fair: present value of benefits would be equal to present value of contributions. There would be no distortion in those accounts. Besides those notional accounts, there would be a redistributive program that would unavoidably be distortionary.

There are several problems with such an approach. First, there is the previously discussed issue of political support of the redistributive scheme.

---

[7] See Sorensen (2003).

Second, it could be used as a first step toward privatization of the notional accounts system along with abandonment of the redistributive scheme. Third, it assumes away the possibility of myopic behavior, which is one of the main reasons for forced saving. Finally, it does not take into account a number of market failures (annuities, long-term care, unemployment insurance) that motivate public action. Let us illustrate the point concerning the perceived contributory factor.

Consider a society comprising two (types of) individuals with wage income $w_2 > w_1 = 0$. The only source of income of individual 1 is a transfer from the government expressed as $P_1 = b$. Individual 2 pays a tax τ on his earnings $w_2 l_2$, where l_2 is labor supply, and receives from the government

$$P_2 = b + \alpha \tau w_2 l_2.$$

The revenue constraint is thus

$$2b = \tau (1 - \alpha) w_2 l_2.$$

With a quadratic disutility of labor, the utilities of both individuals end up to be equal to

$$U_1 = b; U_2 = w_2 l_2 (1 - \tau) - l_2^2/2 + P_2.$$

Individual 2 maximizes his utility with respect to l_2:

$$Max_{l_2}: w_2 l_2 \left[1 - \tau(1 - \alpha^P)\right] + b - l_2^2/2.$$

This implies that $l_2 = w_2 \left[1 - \tau(1 - \alpha^P)\right]$. Assume that $w_2 = 10$, $\tau = 0.2$, $\alpha = 1/2$. We consider three cases of (mis)perception.

1. $\alpha^P = \alpha$. Then $l_2 = 9; b = 4.5$.
2. $\alpha^P = 0$. Then $l_2 = 8; b = 4$.
3. $\alpha^P = 1$. Then $l_2 = 10; b = 5$.

Clearly for individual 1, case 3 is ideal, followed by case 1.

3 Performance of the Welfare State

One of the most widespread critiques leveled against the welfare state is its inefficiency in distributing benefits and in producing services. This section deals with the measurement of performance of the welfare state in providing social services and social transfers. Ideally, the performance of the welfare state as a whole or that of its components can be assessed by the extent to which they fulfill the objectives assigned to them. We will analyze the efficiency of various transfer programs (social security, unemployment insurance), that of production of services (education, health, transportation), and that of the welfare state as a whole.

3.1 Transfer Programs: Administrative Costs and Redistributive Efficiency

A well-functioning transfer program, such as public pensions or health care, is expected to minimize its administrative cost and to allocate benefits to the targeted population. Private and public insurance schemes incur what is called expense loading, that is, the amount covering both administrative and maintenance costs. Compared to the private sector, administrative costs tend to be quite low in the public sector. Two factors explain such a difference: the scale that is much larger in public programs, most often covering the entire population, and the absence of expensive advertising campaigns.

Another problem with social assistance programs is the distributive inefficiency that occurs when needy households do not exercise their right to benefit from them, while other households not suffering from precarious conditions do benefit from them. The first problem is linked to the issue of take-ups caused by ignorance or fear of stigmatization. The second problem that arises when well-off social groups often benefit from social provisions intended for disadvantaged groups has been studied under the name of the "Matthew effect."[8]. Accordingly, for cultural and institutional reasons, well-off individuals outsmart disadvantaged ones to have access to various social programs. One famous example is the use of Medicaid[9] for long-term care by the American middle class through a process of strategic impoverishment. The strategy is standard: spending down to be entitled to means-tested programs.

The Matthew effect is generally considered as bad and thus should be fought against. At the same time, following Korpi and Palme (1998); Korpi and Palme (2003), we have the "paradox of redistribution" according to which it can be desirable to let the middle class benefit from social programs to ensure their political support. In other words, a program that is restricted to the poor has a smaller redistributive effect than universal systems. We dealt with this issue by showing that a social program would benefit from being partially Bismarckian according to the old saying: A program for the poor is a poor program.

So far, the focus is on the efficiency of social transfer programs and their administrative costs. In this particular activity the index of performance is

---

[8] Deleeck (1979), Merton (1968).
[9] Medicaid is the American public health insurance program for people with low income. It covers one in five Americans and rests on means testing.

unidimensional; thus, measuring it is quite easy. The difficulty arises when there are several kinds of services produced or provided, and resources used. We now turn to this problem.

3.2 Productive Efficiency

For an economist, an activity is called productively inefficient if the same production of goods and services can be carried out with fewer resources, or if more can be produced with the resources used. To illustrate this concept, a figure may be helpful. Being restricted to two dimensions, we consider an activity i that produces a service y_i out of an input x_i where i represents country i. This activity could be that of railway transports. Figure 2 represents such an outcome with dots, one for each country i. From this set of observations, one can construct a best practice frontier. On Figure 2a, the curve A is obtained by OLS and curve B is just displaced upward so as to envelop all activities. Only activity C is on the frontier. On Figure 2b, we have the same set of dots, and here the best practice frontier is the broken line that envelops the dots. This broken line represents the productive efficiency frontier. These two best practice frontiers, one obtained through a parametric (econometric) technique and the other through a nonparametric (linear programming) method curve, provide the yardstick with respect to which the efficiency of each activity i can be assessed. The standard nonparametric technique is the Data Envelopment Analysis (DEA) to which we come back. The relative vertical distance between a dot and this frontier measures what we call the productive inefficiency of the activity represented by this dot. Note that such a measure can apply to a setting with multiple outputs and inputs, possibly including quality indicators.

The measuring of productive efficiency would be a rather simple exercise if the efficiency frontier were known. Unfortunately, this is not the case, as the true frontier cannot be found in the blueprints of a social engineer. It must thus be inferred from the reality; that is, constructed from a sample of possibly inefficient observations. The dots shown in Figure 2 represent such a sample. For that reason, the choice of the sample of observations is crucial. It is important that they originate from similar conditions with respect to the technology. To take the case of a cross-section sample of postal services, the question of spatial homogeneity is quite relevant. It is not impossible that geographical or institutional differences go a long way toward explaining variations in performance. Part of the efficiency assessment exercise consists in accounting for these differences. One can see right away the limitations of the efficiency frontier approach for the purpose at hand. First, it only applies to components of the welfare state in which there is production of

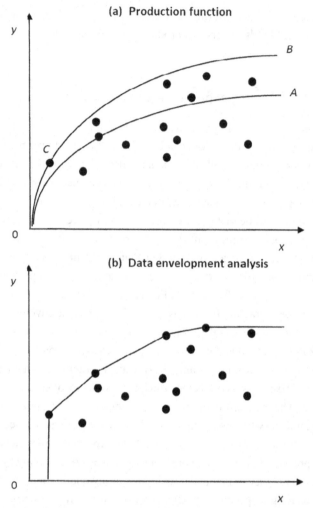

Figure 2 Productive inefficiency: (a) parametric and (b) nonparametric
approach

services: hospitals, garbage collection, and schools. Secondly, since the method
is comparative, it concerns activities with a large number of comparable
productive units.[10]

It is clear that productive efficiency should not be the sole objective of social
policymakers. There are other objectives, for sure: first of all, achieving some
redistribution, as we have seen, but also fostering employment and growth
while keeping aware of the financial constraints. Some of these objectives
are not always compatible. Productive efficiency is, indeed, the only objective

---

[10] For a survey of efficiency studies, see Lefebvre et al. (2017).

whose achievement does not impede the achievement of the other objectives. Producing too few services or employing too many resources, as compared to what is technically feasible, cannot be justified in terms of any of the other objectives traditionally assigned to the welfare state.

3.3 Performance

Public expenditures for education and health are considered as efficient means of redistribution in today's welfare states.[11] Section 3.2 presented some means of assessing their productive efficiency at the "firms" level. Can we apply the same methodology to assess the efficiency of the health or the education sector of a country or a region by using a rough estimate of the outcomes as output and public spending as input? Not really, for a number of reasons, including the fact that the performance of a health or of an education system depends on several factors that are not easily quantifiable and are most often unavailable: for example, the climate, the diet, and the family structure. What we can do in those cases is to measure the performance and not the efficiency of the programs by focusing on a number of indicators that correspond to their basic objectives and without using any output. To see the difference between the concept of efficiency and that of performance, we can use as an analogy the difference between ranking students according to their outcomes (grades) and ranking them according to their merits (grades weighted by social background or handicap). Their performance is measured by their grades and their efficiency by their merits.

To measure the performance of the welfare state, we use five indicators that correspond to the five more important objectives that it is supposed to pursue: poverty alleviation, inequality reduction, full employment, education and training, and finally health.[12] The European Commission publishes every year a set of social indicators that are supposed to induce each member country to improve its performance where it is lagging.[13] We have thus selected the following partial indicators that cover a period of twenty-five years (1995–2019) for the first fifteen EU members. They are

- POV: poverty rate (60 percent of median income)
- INE: interquintile ratios

---

[11] Paulus et al. (2010).

[12] Coelli et al. (2010).

[13] This data is collected within the framework of the open method of coordination (OMC), which is a means of governance in the European Union based on the voluntary cooperation of its member states. The OMC rests on the regular publication of indicators leading to benchmarking and sharing of best practice.

- UNE: long-term unemployment
- EDU: early school leavers
- EXP: life expectancy

To make them comparable, we normalize them from zero to one following the approach used by the United Nations for the HDI (Human Development Indicator). For the first four indicators whose best value is the lowest, we proceed as follows. We take the example of POV_i. The normalized partial indicator of poverty for country i can be written as

$$PI_{POV_i} = \frac{POV^+ - POV_i}{POV^+ - POV^-},$$

where POV^+ and POV^- denote the highest and lowest poverty rate in the sample.

Using the same notation for life expectancy, EXP_i, the partial indicator of country i will be written as

$$PI_{EXP_i} = \frac{EXP_i - EXP^-}{EXP^+ - EXP^-}.$$

Once those partial indicators are normalized, what can we do? A first step is to present them in a pentagonal shape such as the one shown in Figure 3, where we plotted four countries. We could have done that for the twenty-eight EU member countries in 2019, but the results would have been unreadable. Even with just four countries, we can hardly say much, except that Germany dominates the UK and that Spain is weak on four indicators but excellent on life expectancy.

Henceforth, we decide to aggregate those five partial indicators. We resort to two approaches:

- the unweighted sum of partial indicators (SPI)
- distance with respect to a best practice frontier constructed by using the *DEA* approach with a unitary input.

To illustrate those two approaches, we use a simple example with just two partial indicators and six countries. The outcome of each country is presented by a dot in Figure 4. The DEA best practice frontier envelops those points and is given by the broken line $1\alpha\gamma\beta1$. Countries α, β, γ receive the maximum score of one. As to the other countries, their score is given by their relative distance from zero to the best practice frontier. The scores of ε and δ are given by the ratios $0\varepsilon/01$ and $0\delta/01$ respectively.

With the SPI, we just add the two partial indicators weighted by 1/2. To get a score of one, a country would have to be on a dot with coordinates (1, 1). To get the actual SPI score of each country, we draw parallel lines with −1 slopes. The relative distance of one of these lines with the maximum (1,1) gives the

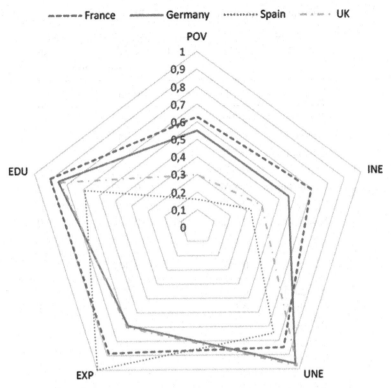

Figure 3 Primary indicators in four countries (2019)

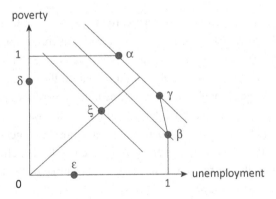

Figure 4 DEA and SPI

score of the country located on this line. For example, the score of ξ is given by the ratio $0\xi/01$ on the main diagonal.

Whereas with the SPI approach each indicator receives the same weight of 20 percent, with the DEA, the weight varies with the partial indicator, the country, and the year. It can be shown that the weight given to an indicator

Table 1 Performance indicators 2019 (EU 28)

	Country	SPI	Ranking	DEA Constrained	Ranking
	Mean	0.774		0.934	
	Finland	0.880	2	1.000	1
	France	0.821	9	0.982	6
	Germany	0.770	13	0.932	14
EU-15	Italy	0.639	23	0.852	21
	Netherlands	0.855	5	0.990	5
	Spain	0.622	24	0.843	22
	Sweden	0.818	10	0.976	9
	UK	0.693	20	0.865	20
	Mean	0.696		0.842	
	Bulgaria	0.436	28	0.510	28
EU-13	Czech R.	0.878	3	1.000	1
	Romania	0.468	27	0.615	27
	Slovakia	0.797	11	0.946	11
	Slovenia	0.888	1	1.000	1
EU-28	Mean	0.738		0.892	

depends on how good a country is with regard to this indicator. In this example, a country with scores of one for poverty and zero for unemployment would get the performance score of one. In our data, this is the case of Spain. Spain would get a score of one, as all the weight would be put on the health indicator, in which it excels, even though it underperforms in the other four indicators (see Figure 3). This is why, in our DEA evaluation, we constrain each indicator to have a weight of at least 10 percent. Using those endogenous weights instead of arbitrary fixed ones is an approach based on the benefit of doubt.[14] Table 1 provides the performance indicators of a sample of the twenty-eight EU member countries in 2019.

This calls for a number of comments. The correlation between SPI and DEA at the EU28 level is 0.972. As the figures show, SPI is lower than DEA. Among the highest scores, one finds countries from Eastern Europe that joined the EU lately. Extension from fifteen countries to twenty-eight did not decrease average performance. The least performing countries are the usual suspects:

---

[14] This term was first used by Cherchye et al. (2010).

Table 2 Relative importance in percentage of the
role of the state, the market, and the family

	State	Market	Family
Long-term care	25	5	70
Health care	70	0	30
Social security	70	5	25

Bulgaria and Romania. Other normalizations yield the same results. For the EU15, the first members of the European Union, one has a series of twenty-five years for either the SPI or the DEA indicator. It appears that both indicators increase over time and converge. This surprising result seems to refute the expectation that economic integration and factor mobility would lead to a race to the bottom and to some social dumping. This finding is naturally contingent on the five indicators we adopted, which do not include the various social divides mentioned earlier.

4 Social Protection and Private Insurance

This fourth section of the Element first looks at the differences and the resemblance between social and private insurance. The main difference is the redistributive mission and the scale of social insurance compared to its private counterparts. Private insurance does not have redistributive purposes and its scale is relatively limited. Both types of insurance share the same concern as to the design of insurance contract and how to cope with moral hazard and adverse selection. Finally, different issues pertaining to public pensions are analyzed.

4.1 The State, the Market, and the Family

Over centuries, social protection has mostly been provided by the (extended) family. The market and then the state appeared only a century ago. The family is still very active in the areas of long-term care and child care. It is interesting to see what is the relative involvement of those three institutions in health, pensions, and long-term care. Taking as a reference countries such as France and Germany, we have a back-of-the-envelope allocation presented in Table 2. It appears clearly that for both health and social security the state dominates, whereas for assistance to dependent elderly the family is still the main provider of care.

Focusing on the formal types of insurance, we observe that spending on social insurance dominates spending on private insurance. This domination is strengthened when taking into account the fact that private insurance is

Table 3 Social versus private insurance

Area	Advantage of social insurance over private insurance
Large risks	High except in case of reinsurance
Intergenerational smoothing	Absolute
Moral hazard	Nil
Adverse selection	High except when insurance is mandatory
Redistribution	Absolute
Administrative costs	High
Financing	Negative
Commitment	Nil
Single provision	High in the field of health care

providing social protection. In percentage of GDP, in the EU, private insurance ranges from 2.0 (Lithuania) to 10.4 (Ireland) and social insurance from 13.4 (Ireland) to 31 (France).[15]

Regarding the pluses and the minuses of the two types of insurance, the pluses for public insurance are the coverage of large risks such as floods, earthquakes or pandemics, intergenerational smoothing, redistribution, low administrative costs, and single provision (see Table 3). The pluses of private insurance are that its financing does not bear any distortion and is not endangered by the race to the bottom. Regarding moral hazard, adverse selection, and commitment, the comparative advantage of one type of insurance over the other is not clear.

A word on the last two items in the table. Private insurers do not make long-term commitments; their contracts are generally annual and renegotiable. The public sector can be committed to a program for a long period, but under political pressure it often has to back down on its previous commitments. As to the single provision issue, countries such as the UK that have a public health system insuring individuals and providing medical services tend to be quite efficient, more so than countries with decentralized provision.

4.2 Redistributive Social Insurance

We now turn to a model that shows why social insurance might be desirable for redistributive purposes even when income taxation is available.[16] The

---

[15] OECD (2020a), OECD (2020b).
[16] See Rochet (1991), Cremer and Pestieau (1996), and Boadway et al. (2003).

reason is that under some plausible assumptions social insurance does not entail distortions while redistributive income taxation does. In this model, individuals of type i are characterized not just by their productivity w_i, but also by their probability p_i of incurring a monetary loss D.[17] There are two types of insurance: private (actuarially fair) and social (redistributive). Given risk aversion and actuarial fairness, there will be full insurance. The question is whether it is to be provided by the government or the market. In the absence of insurance and assuming a linear income tax, we would have a different disposable income in case of accident or when there is no accident:

- $x^{ac} = wl(1 - \tau) + a - D,$
- $x^{na} = wl(1 - \tau) + a,$

where τ and a denote the tax rate and a flat rate transfer. Labor supply is denoted by l.

Assume now that the social insurance covers a fraction α of the damage and that the private insurance covers the rest. We now have just the same disposable income for both states of nature:

$$x_i = x_i^{ac} = x_i^{na} = w_i l_i (1 - \tau) + a - D[(1 - \alpha)p_i + \alpha \bar{p}],$$

where $\bar{p} = \sum_i n_i p_i$.

The utility can be written as

$$U_i = u(x_i) - v(l_i),$$

where $v(l_i)$ is the disutility of labor. Assuming a utilitarian objective and using the FOC for the individual $[u'(x_i)w_i(1 - \tau) = v'(l_i)]$, the problem of the social planner is to maximize

$$\mathcal{L} = \sum n_i \{u[w_i l_i(1 - \tau) + a - D[(1-\alpha)p_i + \alpha p]] - v(l_i) - \mu[a - \tau w_i l_i]\},$$

where μ is the Lagrange multiplier associated with the revenue constraint.

The FOCs with respect to a, τ, α are

$$\frac{\partial \mathcal{L}}{\partial a} = \sum n_i \left[u'(x_i) - \mu \left(1 - \tau w_i \frac{\partial l_i}{\partial a} \right) \right] = 0, \tag{1}$$

$$\frac{\partial \mathcal{L}}{\partial \tau} = \sum n_i \left[-u'(x_i)w_i l_i + \mu \left(w_i l_i - \tau w_i \frac{\partial l_i}{\partial \tau} \right) \right] = 0, \tag{2}$$

$$\frac{\partial \mathcal{L}}{\partial \alpha} = \sum n_i u'(x_i)(p_i - \bar{p})D = cov(u'(x), p) D. \tag{3}$$

[17] In the sections devoted to insurance, p denotes the probability; in the sections devoted to pensions, it denotes the pension benefit.

Focusing first on the FOC (3), we have

$$\frac{\partial \mathcal{L}}{\partial \alpha} > 0 \iff cov\,(u'(x),p) \iff corr(p,w) < 0.$$

In words, it is desirable to increase the share of public insurance up to the maximum possible if the risk of loss is negatively correlated to income. This seems to be the case for most lifetime risks such as disability, unemployment, and sickness.

Turning to the FOCs (1) and (2) and using the notation $Ex = \sum n_i x_i$, we obtain the effect of the tax, compensated by the lump sum transfer, on social welfare. This is given by

$$\frac{\partial \mathcal{L}}{\partial \tau} + \frac{\partial \mathcal{L}}{\partial a} Ewl = -E\,[u'(x)wl] + Eu'(x)Ewl + \mu\tau Ew\frac{\partial l^c}{\partial \tau} = 0,$$

or

$$\tau = \frac{-cov(u'(x),wl)}{-\mu Ew\frac{\partial l^c}{\partial \tau}} > 0, \tag{4}$$

where $\frac{\partial l^c}{\partial \tau} \left(= \frac{\partial l}{\partial \tau} - \frac{\partial l}{\partial a} Ewl\right) < 0$ denotes the compensated effect of the tax on the labor supply. The numerator of the tax formula (4) represents the equity effect of the tax $(cov(u'(x),wl) < 0)$. The size of the equity effect depends on the wage inequality and on the concavity of the utility function. As to the denominator, it reflects the efficiency effect. If the labor supply is inelastic, or in other words, if the tax does not modify the individual behavior much, the tax will tend to be high. In Section 5.2 we will present the nonlinear version of this problem.

4.3 Coinsurance or Deductible

We now move to the design of an insurance contract and the issue of whether we should opt for a contract based on coinsurance or on deductible. We keep in mind Arrow's underrated deductible theorem. This theorem states that, if an insurance company is willing to offer any insurance policy against loss desired by the buyer at a premium that depends only on the policy's actuarial value, then the policy chosen by a risk-averting buyer will take the form of 100 percent coverage above a deductible minimum.[18] This theorem rests on the existence of loading costs. Otherwise, there would be a 100 percent insurance coverage. It implies that an insurance with deductible dominates the more traditional policy based on coinsurance rates.

Following Drèze and Schokkaert (2013) we consider a simple example with S states of nature. The variable A_s is the initial health status that decreases

---

[18] Arrow (1963).

with s $(s - 1, 2, ..., S)$. The final health status is denoted by $m_s = A_s + d_s$, where d_s represents the level of medical expenditures and at the same time the improvement in health. The individual has a given income w and a utility U_s that depends on consumption c_s and health m_s. The insurance rate is α_s, the insurance premium π, and the loading factor λ. The rate of coinsurance is thus $1 - \alpha_s$. A direct application of this model is sickness or dependence. As s increases, the severity of sickness grows or the number of months of dependence augments.

We first analyze the case where health spending is observable and then the case where it is not observable and can thus be influenced by the rate of reimbursement, which is the case with ex post moral hazard.[19]

4.3.1 No Moral Hazard

Individual utility is given by

$$U_s = u(c_s) + h(m_s)$$

or

$$U_s = u(w - \pi - (1 - \alpha_s)\, d_s) + h(A_s + d_s).$$

The insurance premium is defined as

$$\pi = (1 + \lambda) \sum_t^S p_t \alpha_t d_t.$$

We can now write the problem to be solved, namely finding the values of d_s and α_s that maximize the following expected utility (denoted by $\mathcal{L}$):

$$\mathcal{L} = \sum_s^S p_s \left[u\!\left(w - (1 + \lambda) \sum_t^S p_t \alpha_t d_t - (1 - \alpha_s)\, d_s\right) + h(A_s + d_s) \right].$$

We obtain the FOCs:

$$\frac{\partial \mathcal{L}}{\partial d_s} = -u'(c_s)\,(1 - \alpha_s) + h'(m_s) - (1 + \lambda)\alpha_s \sum p_t u'(c_t) = 0,$$

$$\frac{\partial \mathcal{L}}{\partial \alpha_s} = d_s \left[u'(c_s) - (1 + \lambda) \sum p_t u'(c_t) \right] \leq 0.$$

This implies

$$u'(c_s) = h'(m_s)$$

---

[19] In insurance economics, we distinguish between ex ante and ex post moral hazard. Ex ante moral hazard is a change in behavior prior to the outcome of the random event. Ex post moral hazard involves behavior after the outcome.

and we distinguish between two regimes of light and heavy sickness according to the value of s with respect to a threshold value $\bar{s}$:

$$s < \bar{s} \Rightarrow \frac{\partial \mathcal{L}}{\partial \alpha_s} < 0 \Longrightarrow \alpha_s = 0$$

and

$$s > \bar{s} \Rightarrow \frac{\partial \mathcal{L}}{\partial \alpha_s} = 0 \Longrightarrow u'(c_s) = (1 + \lambda) \sum p_t u'(c_t) \Longrightarrow (1 - \alpha_s) d_s = F.$$

In other words, for any expense below F there is no coverage. For any expense above F, there is full coverage. F is the deductible.

Note that if $\lambda = 0$, $\alpha_s = 1$ and there is full coverage of any expense.

4.3.2 Moral Hazard

We now introduce the possibility of ex post moral hazard. Now spending is not observable and is chosen by the individual, given the value of α. This amounts to

$$Max_{d_s} = u(w - \pi - (1 - \alpha_s) d_s) + h(A_s + d_s).$$

The FOC is

$$-u'(c_s)(1 - \alpha_s) + h'(m_s) = 0.$$

We thus have $d(\alpha_s)$ with $\frac{\partial d_s}{\partial \alpha_s} > 0$. The problem of the insurer is thus to find the values of α_s that maximize

$$\mathcal{L} = \sum p_s \left[u(w - (1 + \lambda) \sum p_t \alpha_t d_t - (1 - \alpha_s) d_s) + h(A_s + d_s) \right].$$

The solution is not necessarily interior, and the FOC is written as

$$\frac{\partial \mathcal{L}}{\partial \alpha_s} = \left[-u'(c_s)(1 - \alpha_s) + h'(m_s) - (1 + \lambda)\alpha_s \sum p_t u'(c_t) \right] \frac{\partial d_s}{\partial \alpha_s}$$
$$+ d_s \left[u'(c_s) - (1 + \lambda) \sum p_t u'(c_t) \right] \leq 0$$

or

$$\frac{\partial \mathcal{L}}{\partial \alpha_s} = d_s u'(c_s) - \left[(1 - \alpha_s) u'(c_s) \frac{\partial d_s}{\partial \alpha_s} - h'(m_s) \frac{\partial d_s}{\partial \alpha_s} \right]$$
$$- \left[d_s + \frac{\partial d_s}{\partial \alpha_s} \frac{\alpha_s}{d_s} \right] (1 + \lambda)(1 + \eta_s) \sum p_t u'(c_t) \leq 0.$$

After simplification, we obtain

$$\frac{\partial \mathcal{L}}{\partial \alpha_s} = d_s \left[u'(c_s) - (1 + \lambda)(1 + \eta_s) \sum p_t u'(c_t) \right] \leq 0,$$

where $\eta_s = \frac{\alpha_s \partial d_s}{d_s \partial \alpha_s} > 0$. If $\eta_s = \bar{\eta}$ is constant, c_s is constant and the deductible is $(1 - \alpha_s) d_s = F$ with $\frac{dF}{d\bar{\eta}} > 0$. Whether this elasticity is constant is an empirical question.[20]

4.3.3 Coinsurance and Moral Hazard

We now turn to a simpler model with two states of nature: 0 for healthy and 1 for sick. We want to show that the insurance rate depends on two main terms: the moral hazard effect, and the insurance effect, which depends on risk aversion combined with the degree of uncertainty. The utility function is

$$U = p\left[u(c_1) + h(A + d)\right] + (1 - p)\left[u(c_0) + h(A^*)\right],$$

where $c_1 = w - d(1 - \alpha) - \pi$ and $c_0 = w - \pi$. Further, $A < A^*$.

There are two stages. In the first, the individual chooses d for a given α. This yields the FOC:

$$u'(c_1)(1 - \alpha) = h'(A + d).$$

This yields the demand function $d(\alpha)$ with $d'(\alpha) > 0$. In the second stage, the insurance agent chooses α to maximize U subject to the revenue constraint:

$$\pi = (1 + \lambda)\alpha p d.$$

The utility can be rewritten as

$$U = p\left[u(w - d(1 - \alpha) - (1 + \lambda)\alpha p d) + h(A + d)\right]$$
$$+ (1 - p)\left[u(w - (1 + \lambda)\alpha p d) + h(A^*)\right].$$

The FOC is

$$p\left[u'(c_1)(d - (1 - \alpha)d'(\alpha) - (1 + \lambda)p(d + \alpha d'(\alpha)) + h'(A + d)d'(\alpha)\right]$$
$$+ (1 - p)\left[-u'(c_0)(1 + \lambda)p(d + \alpha d'(\alpha))\right] = 0.$$

From the envelope theorem, this can be rewritten as

$$pu'(c_1)\left[(d - (1 + \lambda)p(d + \alpha d'(\alpha))\right]$$
$$+ (1 - p)\left[-u'(c_0)(1 + \lambda)p(d + \alpha d'(\alpha))\right] = 0.$$

From this latter condition, we obtain the formula for the insurance rate:

$$\alpha = \frac{(1 - p)\left[u'(c_1) - u'(c_0)\right] - \frac{\lambda}{(1+\lambda)}u'(c_1)}{\frac{d'(\alpha)}{d(\alpha)}\left[pu'(c_1) + (1 - p)u'(c_0)\right]}.$$

---

[20] See, on this, Einav and Finkelstein (2018).

With no loading cost, this expression reduces to

$$\alpha = \frac{(1-p)\,[u'(c_1) - u'(c_0)]}{\frac{d'(\alpha)}{d(\alpha)}\,[pu'(c_1) + (1-p)u'(c_0)]}.$$

The rate of insurance increases with the concavity of $u(c)$, the utility function (risk aversion) and decreases with the loading cost λ and the extent of moral hazard $[d'(\alpha)]$.

It should be noted that with just two states of nature (healthy or sick), coinsurance and deductible coincide. In the case of disease, the insuree is subject to a deductible $F = (1-\alpha)d$. He pays this deductible and gets compensated for αd from the insurance scheme.

4.4 Adverse Selection

In Section 4.3, we dealt with the case where the public or the private insurer was not able to observe the level of spending. We now turn to the case where the individual probabilities of loss are not observable. We then face the problem of adverse selection that can be solved either by making insurance mandatory or by self-selecting the individuals in such a way that the good (low-) risk individuals are only partially covered.[21] Otherwise, there is no equilibrium. Consider two types of individuals denoted L and H where L stands for low-risk and H for high-risk. They have the same initial wealth w, incur the risk of an identical monetary loss D, but differ in the probability of incurring this loss with $p_l < p_h$. Their expected utility is given by

$$U_i = p_i u(w - D) + (1 - p_i)u(w) = p_i u(w_2) + (1 - p_i)u(w_1),$$

where $i = h, l$ and the subscript 1 (2) denotes the state of the world without (with) loss. We can represent by E in Figure 5 the allocation implied by this loss: $E = (w - D, w)$. The coordinates w_1 and w_2 denote respectively final wealth without and with the loss.

Let us introduce an actuarially fair insurance. Two types of equilibria can occur. First, we can have a pooling equilibrium with full coverage and an insurance premium $\bar{p}D$ where $\bar{p} = \sum_{l,h} n_i p_i$ and n_i is the fraction of individuals of type $i = l, h$. In that case the resulting allocation is given by the vector: $F = w - \bar{p}D$, the same for both H and L. Note that all allocations to the left of EF are such that the insurer makes a gain; those to right imply a loss. Second, we can have separating equilibria given by $F^H = w - p_h D$ and $F^L = w - p_l D$.

[21] Rothschild and Stiglitz (1976).

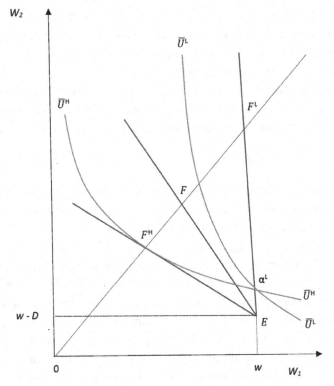

Figure 5 Adverse selection

As shown on Figure 5 and easily verified analytically,[22] the indifference curve of H is flatter than that of L. This implies that the pooling equilibrium F is not sustainable. Individual L will always find desirable to opt for a different preferable insurance contract. The only way to implement it would be to make it compulsory.

The separating equilibria F^L and F^H are not sustainable because the individual H will be tempted to mimic individual L to get a more attractive allocation. To avoid that, we have to restrict the coverage of individual L such that his allocation is given by α^L. One clearly sees that then individual H does not have any incentive to mimic L. Note that the lines EF^L, EF, and EF^H correspond to the different insurance coverage with probabilities $p_l, \bar{p}$, and p_h. For example, the line EF^L has a slope equal to $\frac{1-p_l}{p_l}$. Denoting the insurance rate by β, we have that $\alpha^L = (w_1^L, w_2^L)$, where $w_1^L = w - \beta p_l D$ and $w_2^L = w - \beta p_l D - (1 - \beta)D$. As β increases from 0 to 1, w_1 and w_2 move from E to F^L. The allocation α^L implies a particular value of β, an insurance rate that is

---

22 $\frac{dw_2}{dw_1} = -\frac{(1-p)u'(w_1)}{pu'(w_2)}$.

low enough to discourage type H's individuals to mimic type L's individuals. This separating equilibrium is not necessarily stable. In the example of Figure 5, it is stable because any other allocation preferred by the two types of agents would not be profitable to the insurer.

Note that the pooling solution generates some redistribution from types L to types H. In the situations where types L happen to have a higer income than types H, this redistribution is clearly socially desirable, as we have seen earlier.

4.5 Pensions and Annuities

In most OECD countries, the bulk of retirement income comes from public schemes. Public pensions have been under scrutiny for a number of reasons pertaining mainly to their sustainability.

First, there is the critique that pension systems in a number of countries induce early retirement, which makes their financing difficult. Second, there is the critique that public pensions that are based on the defined benefit principle put all the burden of financial or demographic shocks on the shoulders of the active population. Third, there is the charge against the pay-as-you go systems that they hurt capital accumulation. At the same time, it is not easy to revert to a fully funded rule, as this would involve either sacrificing the transition generation or issuing a debt that would have the same effect as a pay-as-you-go (PAYGO) pension. Finally, with the development of defined contribution plans[23] in private but also public pensions, the availability of affordable annuities become more and more relevant.

4.5.1 Early Retirement

We start with the two-period model with endogenous retirement age that was introduced in Section 2.1. Denoting by s the level of saving and by z the fraction of the second period devoted to work, the individual utility is given by

$$U = u(w(1 - \tau) - s) + \beta u((1 + r)s + p(z) + wz(1 - \tau) - z^2/2),$$

where $p(z)$ denotes the total amount of pension that is going to be granted to the retiree. The pension does depend on the length of the working career $(1 + z)$. We adopt a quadratic specification for the disutility of work. Maximizing this utility with respect to the age of retirement yields

$$z = p'(z) + w(1 - \tau) = w(1 - \theta),$$

---

[23] Unlike a defined benefit (DB) plan, a defined contribution (DC) plan does not promise a specific amount of benefits at retirement, but sets a rate of contribution to be paid by the employers or the employees (or both).

where $\theta = \tau - p'(z)/w$ is the implicit tax on prolonged activity. We can distinguish different cases:

- $\theta = 0$: neutrality (Japan)
- $\theta = \tau$: overall pension payments independent of the age of retirement (USA)
- $\theta = \tau + \bar{p}/w$ if constant annual pension: $p(z) = \bar{p}(1 - z)$ (France)

There is a lot of evidence showing the negative correlation between the effective age of retirement and the implicit tax on postponed activity.[24] The implicit tax explains why the Japanese retire late and the French and the Italians retire early. In Section 2.1, we showed that with a Bismarckian scheme, there is no distortion in the choice of z. Here we obtain the same outcome with a scheme that is designed in such a way that the implicit tax is nil.

4.5.2 Defined Benefit versus Defined Contribution

We assume that both the rate of interest and the time preference are nil and that the wage rate, w, is given and constant.

The pension system is PAYGO. We focus on demographic changes. We distinguish between two regimes: defined benefits (DB) and defined contributions (DC). They imply the following revenue constraints:

- $L_t p_{t+1} = L_{t+1}\tau$ (DC),
- $L_t p = L_{t+1}\tau_{t+1}$ (DB),

where $L_{t+1} = (1 + n_{t+1})L_t$ denotes the size of the working generation in period $t + 1$.

This can also be written as

- $p_{t+1} = (1 + n_{t+1})\tau$ (DC),
- $p = \tau_{t+1}(1 + n_{t+1})$ (DB).

Consider a steady state with $n = 0$ and thus $p = \tau$. At time $t + 1$ the rate of growth of population falls below 0. With DC, the pensioners of generation t will have a lower pension than expected. With DB, the worker of generation $t + 1$ will have to pay a higher payroll tax than anticipated.

If the shocks last just one period $(t + 1)$, with DB, the loser is generation $t + 1$, and with DC, the loser will be generation t.

To avoid those extreme outcomes, it was suggested by Richard Musgrave (1981) to adopt a combination of DB and DC so as to smooth the burden of

---

[24] Gruber and Wise (1999).

shocks on at least two generations.[25] More explicitly, the Musgrave rule states that a pension system is intergenerationally fair if the ratio of per capita benefits to retirees to per capita earnings of workers (net of social security tax) is fixed. This replacement ratio is equal to $\frac{p_t}{w_t - \tau_t}$.

4.5.3 PAYGO and Capital Accumulation

We consider an overlapping generation model.[26] At time 1, the generation 1 is active and the generation 0 is retired. For whatever reasons, generation 1 decides to contribute τ to finance generation 0's pension, $p = \tau(1 + n)$, and to commit society to such a scheme. The rate of population growth is n, which implies that there are $1 + n$ more active individuals than inactive ones. We want to show the following:

- Such a scheme depresses capital accumulation.
- Any attempt to revert to a fully funded system in which $p = (1 + r)\tau$ at time t^* implies that the generation $t^* - 1$ has no pension, which is not politically nor ethically sustainable.
- If instead of financing the pension of generation 0, the government would have issued a debt equal to p, the outcome would have been the same: servicing the debt or the PAYGO system is equivalent.

Throughout the analysis we implicitly assume that $r > n$; in other words, we are on the good side of the Golden Rule,[27] implying that less capital accumulation is undesirable.

Individual Problem   Each (identical) member of generation t maximizes the following utility:

$$U = u(w_t - \tau - s_t) + \beta u(s_t(1 + r_{t+1}) + \tau(1 + n))$$

or, with log functions,

$$U = \log(w_t - \tau - s_t) + \beta \log(s_t(1 + r_{t+1}) + \tau(1 + n)).$$

The FOC with respect to s_t yields

$$\frac{1}{(w_t - \tau - s_t)} = \beta \frac{1 + r_{t+1}}{s_t(1 + r_{t+1}) + \tau(1 + n)}$$

---

[25] See the appendix for a numerical illustration.

[26] See the appendix for an extensive presentation.

[27] The Golden Rule of capital accumulation corresponds to the maximization of the steady state utility. In the standard model, it is reached when the productivity of capital is equal to the rate of growth of population.

or

$$s_t(1 + r_{t+1}) + \tau(1 + n) = \beta(1 + r_{t+1})(w_t - \tau - s_t).$$

We can thus express the amount of saving explicitly:

$$s_t = \frac{\beta(1 + r_{t+1})(w_t - \tau) - \tau(1 + n)}{(1 + r_{t+1})(1 + \beta)} = \frac{\beta}{1 + \beta}\left[w_t - \tau - \tau\frac{1 + n}{(1 + r_{t+1})\beta}\right].$$

Note that if instead of introducing a PAYGO pension p in time 0, we had financed the pension by public borrowing b to be reimbursed by issuing a debt, we would have the same formula as the preceding one with b substituting for τ.

Production Side   We adopt a Cobb–Douglas production function such that $Y = K^\alpha L^{1-\alpha}$, where Y is aggregate output, K the capital stock, and L is the labor force, which is also the size of the working generation. Population grows at a constant rate n such that $L_{t+1} = L_t(1 + n)$. In intensive form, this can be expressed as $y = k^\alpha$, where $y = Y/L$ and $k = K/L$. Profit maximization in period t implies

$$1 + r_t = \alpha k_t^{\alpha-1}; w_t = (1 - \alpha)k_t^\alpha.$$

Market Equilibrium   The market solution leads to the equality between the demand and the supply of capital. Namely

$$(1 + n)k_{t+1} = s_t = \frac{\beta}{1 + \beta}\left[(1 - \alpha)k_t^\alpha - \tau - \tau\frac{1 + n}{\alpha\beta}k_{t+1}^{1-\alpha}\right].$$

Clearly, k_{t+1} decreases with τ.

The steady state k^* exists and is unique with this specification, and one can show that

$$\frac{dk^*}{d\tau} < 0.$$

In this simple example, the Golden Rule capital stock $\hat{k}$ is such that

$$\alpha\hat{k}^{1-\alpha} = 1 + \hat{r} = 1 + n.$$

We have assumed that $k^* < \hat{k}$.

4.6 The Annuities Market Puzzle with Loading Cost and Bequest Motive

Annuities are considered as the "forgotten half" of retirement security that allows for carefully planning the "payout phase." This is an area where the government does better than the market. For Yaari (1965), under certain conditions, individuals should convert 100 percent of their wealth into annuities. These conditions are

- no bequest motives,
- actuarially fair annuities,
- utility of consumption is additively separable over time, and
- no uncertainty other than date of death.

We now show that when there is a bequest motive and/or there is no actuarial fairness, then it makes sense not to purchase annuities.

Assume that the individual can choose both the level of his saving, s, and the fraction α that he is going to invest in annuities. His survival probability is denoted p. Let us further denote the loading cost of the annuity by λ. The problem is then to choose the values of α and s so as to maximize

$$U = u(w - s) + \beta pu\left[s(1 + r)\left(\frac{\alpha}{p(1 + \lambda)} + (1 - \alpha)\right)\right].$$

The two FOCs are

$$-u'(c) + \beta pu'(d)(1 + r)\left(\frac{\alpha}{p(1 + \lambda)} + (1 - \alpha)\right) = 0$$

and

$$\frac{\partial U}{\partial \alpha} = \beta pu'(d)s(1 + r)\left[\frac{1}{p(1 + \lambda)} - 1\right].$$

This implies that $\alpha = 0$ if $\pi(1 + \lambda) > 1$. To the contrary, $\alpha = 1$ if $p(1 + \lambda) < 1$. Then all the saving is invested in annuity.

Assume now that the individual attaches some value to the bequest he would leave in case of early death. Then we have

$$U = u(w - s) + \beta u\left[s(1 + r)\left(\frac{\alpha}{p(1 + \lambda)} + (1 - \alpha)\right)\right] + \beta(1 - p)v((1 + r)(1 - \alpha)s),$$

where $v(.)$ is the utility one gets from bequeathing and $b = (1 + r)(1 - \alpha)s$ is the amount of unplanned bequests.

The FOC with respect to α is now

$$\frac{\partial U}{\partial \alpha} = \beta s(1 + r)\left[pu'(d)\left(\frac{1}{p(1 + \lambda)} - 1\right) - (1 - p)v'(b)\right].$$

One sees right away that the value of α is lower with this bequest motive and can even be 0. We have thus shown that when annuities are not actuarially fair or when there is a bequest motive, individuals do not convert 100 percent of their wealth into annuities.

5 Social Policies under Asymmetric Information

This fifth section looks at the issue of asymmetric information that is central in the design of social programs. If the social planner were able to observe the characteristics of individuals and to control their behavior, its task would be relatively easy and first-best efficient. In reality, its information is imperfect and one has to resort to second-best solutions such as workfare or tagging that otherwise would not be acceptable.

5.1 Optimal Redistribution

What is the best way of transferring resources from the well-to-do to those who have less? The first-best solution is clearly to resort to a lump sum transfer that does not interfere with the choices of agents (labor supply, saving, education, health). This requires full information as to the characteristics of individuals. When this is not possible, the second-best solution is to rely on optimal income taxation. Such a tax entails distortions but less than indirect taxes. Indeed it makes indirect taxes superfluous under some conditions (separability between labor and consumption and just one unobserved characteristic). When these conditions are not met, then indirect taxation along with income taxation turn out to be desirable. The typical example is social insurance when there are two unknown characteristics: not only labor productivity but also loss probability.

Policies such as in-kind transfers, tagging, and workfare are generally considered as undesirable and inefficient. Cash transfers dominate in-kind transfers, as they let people freely choose their consumption basket. Tagging implies treating identical people differently. Workfare implies wasting resources. However, in particular cases of asymmetric information, these three policies can become desirable.

Before proceeding, some remarks are in order. In looking for the optimal design of public policy, public economists tend to assign to the social planner a utilitarian objective. In most cases, this is a fairly good option. There are, however, cases where utilitarianism is questionable. The first case is when lifetime is uncertain. Take the two-period setting with uncertainty on the second period. At the start, everybody is alike with an endowment of w and a survival probability of p. The expected utility is

$$U = u(c) + pu(d).$$

A utilitarian social planner will maximize the sum of utilities subject to the constraint that $c + pd = w$. This implies that a fraction p of individuals ends up with a utility $U = 2u(\bar{c})$ and a fraction $1 - p$ with $U = u(\bar{c})$, where $\bar{c} = w/(1+p)$. This outcome can be deemed unfair for the unlucky short-lived individuals. An alternative objective could be to assign everyone a first-period consumption w implying the equality of utility between the short- and the long-lived individuals granted that $u(0) = 0$.

Another objection to a static utilitarian approach is that it focuses on present welfare and overlooks the concern that one can have for social mobility. Take two different individuals who live two periods with certainty. We consider two settings. In the first, the consumption vector (c, d) of individual 1 is $(4, 4)$ and that of individual 2 is $(6, 6)$. In the second setting these vectors are respectively $(3, 7)$ and $(7, 3)$. Focusing on social welfare in each period, a utilitarian planner will prefer setting 1 over 2 as $2[u(4) + u(6)] > 2[u(3) + u(7)]$. If we are concerned by mobility, setting 2 might be preferable, as it gives the same outcome to both individuals.

5.2 Income Redistribution and Social Insurance

In Section 4.2, we show that social insurance can be an efficient instrument of redistribution along with a linear income tax. Here we extend this idea to the case with a nonlinear income tax. We consider a society comprising individuals A and D. Individual A is more productive than individual D and has a lower probability of incurring a monetary loss of D ($p_A < p_D$). Assuming actuarially fair private insurance, we can write the utility of each individual as

$$U_i = u(z_i - D[\alpha \bar{p} + (1 - \alpha)p_i]) - v(y_i/w_i),$$

where $y_i = w_i l_i$ is gross income and z_i is disposable income. We assume that A wants to mimic D and thus the second-best problem can be written as the following Lagrangian:

$$\mathcal{L} = \sum_{i=A,D} [u(z_i - D[\alpha \bar{p} + (1 - \alpha)p_i]) - v(y_i/w_i) - \mu (z_i - y_i)]$$
$$+ \lambda [u(z_A - D[\alpha \bar{p} + (1 - \alpha)p_A]) - v(y_A/w_A)$$
$$- u(z_D - D[\alpha \bar{p} + (1 - \alpha)p_A]) + v(y_D/w_A)],$$

where λ is the multiplier associated with the self-selection constraint that the utility of A telling the truth is at least higher than that obtained in case A mimics D.

The FOC with respect to α is

$$\frac{\partial \mathcal{L}}{\partial \alpha} = \sum [u'(c_i)D(p_i - \bar{p})] + \lambda D(p_A - \bar{p})(u'(c_A) - u'(\tilde{c}_A)) > 0,$$

where $\tilde{c}_A = z_D - D[\alpha \bar{p} + (1 - \alpha)p_A] < c_A$ is the consumption of the mimicker. This means that $\alpha = 1$.

As to the FOCs with respect to z_i and y_i:

$$u'(c_A)(1 + \lambda) - \mu = 0; \quad -\frac{v'(y_A/w_A)}{w_A}(1 + \lambda) + \mu = 0,$$

$$u'(c_D) + \lambda u'(\overline{c}_A) - \mu = 0; \quad -\frac{v'(y_D/w_D)}{w_D} + \lambda \frac{v'(y_D/w_A)}{w_A} + \mu = 0.$$

There is no tax on earnings for A and there is one for D as it appears from

$$\frac{v'(l_A)}{u'(c_A)} = w_A; \quad \frac{v'(l_D)}{u'(c_D)} < w_D.$$

We now show that in particular cases we have to depart from basic principles and apply in-kind transfers, tagging, and workfare for lack of information. For convenience, these three cases are dealt with different social objectives:

- in-kind transfers for equal utilities,
- tagging for an utilitarian objective, and
- workfare for reaching the poverty line.

5.3 Transfer in Kind

Let us first look at the case of in-kind transfers.[28] We have two types of individuals, A for able and D for disabled. Type D suffers from some type of disease that implies a loss of utility. That loss can partially be offset by some medical treatment. The goal of the social planner is to equate the utilities of those two individuals. These are simply

- $u_A = y_A$, and
- $u_D = y_D - e^{1-z}$,

where y_i denotes consumption and z the medical treatment that takes the two values of zero or one. The loss of utility due to the disease is denoted e^{1-z} so that it is $e = 2.72$ without treatment and 1 in case of treatment.

Total resources are equal to six. Assuming that only D uses z, the revenue constraint is thus

$$y_A + y_D + z = 6.$$

We now consider three possible solutions.

5.3.1 First-Best: Full Information as to Who Is Who

In this case, one unit of treatment brings more utility than one unit of consumption and thus $z = 1$. The optimal solution is thus to find the value of y_i such that

$$y_A = 5 - y_D = y_D - 1 \Rightarrow y_D = 3 \Rightarrow u_A = u_D = 2.$$

---

[28] Blackorby and Donaldson (1988); Cremer and Gahvari (1997).

5.3.2 Third-Best: Equal Sharing

Assume now that the social planner does not know who is disabled. Then, an easy solution is to give 3 units to each. The resulting allocation implies

$$u_A = 3 > u_D = 1.$$

Individual D devotes 1 unit to medical treatment and is left with 2 units minus the disutility of being sick but treated.

5.3.3 Second-Best with Self-Selection Constraint

Given that individual A will never use the medical treatment, even if provided freely, the government can decide to offer it freely, knowing that only individual D will use it. The choice of consumption is going to be constrained by the self-selection constraint according to which individual A has no incentive to mimic individual D. The self-selection constraint reduces to

$$y_A \geq y_D.$$

Thus the solution is

$$u_A = 2.5; u_D = 1.5.$$

This solution is clearly preferable to the previous one from the standpoint of individual D. Note that to get this result it is essential that the publicly suppled good z is of no interest to individual A. The three solutions are depicted in Figure 6, where the axes are the utilities of both A and D. The first-best is given by A, the second-best by B, and the third-best by C.

5.4 Optimal Redistributive Taxation with Tagging

We now turn to the issue of tagging[29] as a means of redistribution. Again, we use a simple two-individual setting focusing on the redistribution between skilled individuals and individuals with zero productivity. Just a fraction γ of those disabled individuals have a visible handicap. The others cannot be distinguished from the skilled individuals. We consider three cases: first-best with perfect information as to the types; second-best where one can tag those with visible handicaps; third-best where one does not want to distinguish the two types of disabled individuals (for legal or moral reasons). In this section, the objective of the central planner is utilitarian, namely the maximization of the sum of utilities. The utilities are given by

---

[29] Akerlof (1978).

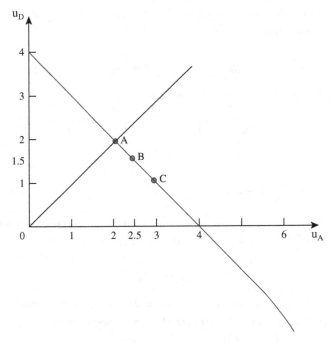

Figure 6 In-kind transfers. Three solutions.

- $u_A = \log c_A - \varepsilon$,
- $u_D = \log c_D$,

where ε denotes the disutility of working, which only concerns individual A. For further use, we posit that $w_D = 0; w_A = 10; \varepsilon = 0.176; 10^\varepsilon = 1.5$.

5.4.1 First-Best

The problem is to maximize the utilitarian social welfare function *SW*:

$$SW = \log c_A - \varepsilon + \log c_D - \mu \left[c_A + c_D - w_A \right].$$

The FOC implies that

$$c_A = c_D = \frac{w_A}{2} = 5.$$

This first-best solution is not sustainable if the social planner cannot sort out the different individuals. It would indeed be tempting for A to mimic D, namely not working and making 5 without suffering the pain of working. To avoid this, we introduce the self-selection constraint:

$$\log c_A - \varepsilon \geq \log c_D.$$

This leads us to the third-best solution (third because the two types of disabled are not distinguished).

5.4.2 Third-Best (or Second-Best without Tagging)

The problem of the social planner now is to maximize

$$SW = \log c_A - \varepsilon + \log c_D - \mu\left[c_A + c_D - w_A\right] + \lambda\left[\log c_A - \varepsilon - \log c_D\right].$$

The FOC is now

$$1 + \lambda = \mu c_A; 1 - \lambda = \mu c_D.$$

This implies that $c_A > c_D$. In fact, from the self-selection constraint we have that $c_A/c_D = 10^\varepsilon = 1.5$. In other words: $c_A = 6; c_D = 4$.

5.4.3 Second-Best

We now show that social welfare will increase if tagging is allowed. This means that the tagged disabled (denoted T) are going to be better treated than the untagged ones, who have to pay the informational penalty. Conversely, individuals A benefit from an informational premium. The problem of the social planner is now to maximize

$$SW = \log c_A - \varepsilon + (1 - \gamma)\log c_D + \gamma \log c_T - \mu\left[c_A + (1 - \gamma)c_D + \gamma c_T - w_A\right]$$
$$+ \lambda\left[\log c_A - \varepsilon - \log c_D\right].$$

We now have three FOCs:

$$1 + \lambda = \mu c_A; 1 = \mu c_T: 1 - \frac{\lambda}{1 - \gamma} = \mu c_D.$$

Using the resource constraint, we obtain

$$2 = \mu w_A \Rightarrow \mu = 0.2.$$

Further, using the fact that $\frac{c_A}{c_D} = 1.5$, we have

$$\lambda = \frac{1 - \gamma}{5 - 2\gamma}.$$

Thus if $\gamma = 0.5$, $\lambda = 0.125$ and we have $c_A = 5.625; c_D = 3.75; c_T = 5$. From the viewpoint of the poorest, the third-best is preferable over the second-best, but with the utilitarian criterion, social welfare is higher with the second-best. These solutions are presented in Table 4.

Table 4 Alternative settings for the tagging problem

Settings/outcomes	y_A	y_T	y_D	Sum of utilities
Laissez-faire	10	0	0	$-\infty$
First-best	5	5	5	$1.3978\text{-}\varepsilon$
Second-best without tagging: $(\gamma = 0)$	6	4	4	$1.3801\text{-}\varepsilon$
Second-best with tagging: $(\gamma = 0.5)$	5.625	5	3.75	$1.3865\text{-}\varepsilon$

5.5 Workfare

Workfare is a government scheme under which people who receive welfare and are able to work must work.[30] The nature of the work is not important, and the motivation can be to maintain the productive capacity or to deter workers from abusing the system. It is considered by some as demeaning and happens to be quite costly.

Again we have two types of individuals with different productivity. The goal of the government is to ensure that the unskilled obtain at least a level of consumption equal to z (poverty line).

Both individuals A and D have a quadratic disutility of labor. Their utility for consumption and labor is simply

$$U_i = y_i - l_i^2/2 = w_i l_i - l_i^2/2.$$

Given that the optimal labor supply is $l_i = w_i$, we have

$$U_i = w_i^2/2.$$

We assume that the wage of the unskilled is such that he cannot reach the poverty line:

$$z > w_D l_D = w_D^2.$$

Again we consider three cases: perfect information with welfare payment b^* (first-best), imperfect information and a uniform welfare payment b^u (third-best), and imperfect information with workfare and welfare benefit b^w (second-best). We show that under certain plausible assumptions the third case is to be preferred to the second one.

---

[30] Besley and Coate (1992).

5.5.1 First-Best

The government observes who are unskilled and provides them with a compensation:

$$b^* = z - w_D^2.$$

The cost of this scheme is $C^* = n_D b^*$.

5.5.2 Second-Best with Uniform Transfer

We now assume that the skilled can mimic the unskilled and benefit from b^u. This scheme costs $C^u = (n_D + n_A)\left(z - w_D^2\right) = z - w_D^2 > C^*$.

5.5.3 Second-Best with Workfare

We now impose to any welfare recipients to devote a amount of time c to some undefined public work. This means that the unskilled earn less than before, implying a higher benefit b^w, but in compensation the skilled will be deterred from getting it. In other words, we will have to compare $C^u = b^u$ and $C^w = n_D b^w$. We thus have:

$$b^w = z - w_D\left(l_D - c\right) = z - w_D^2 + w_D c > b^*.$$

This comes from the optimal choice of l_D:

$$Max: w_D\left(l_D - c\right) - l_D^2/2.$$

We have to find c and b^w that satisfy the self-selection constraint according to which the welfare of individuals A is not lower if they reveal their type than if they mimic individuals D. This is expressed by

$$w_A^2/2 \geq w_A\left(l_A - c\right) - l_A^2/2 + b^w.$$

Assuming that the constraint is binding, we have

$$w_A^2/2 = w_A^2/2 - cw_A + b^w.$$

Hence, using the definition of b^w:

$$0 = -cw_A + b^w = -cw_A + z - w_D^2 + w_D c.$$

We then obtain the value of c that satisfies the self-selection constraint:

$$c^* = \frac{z - w_D^2}{w_A - w_D}.$$

We can now compare the costs of those two schemes, namely whether $C^u \gtrless C^w$. We have

$$C^u = z - w_D^2 = c^*\left(w_A - w_D\right) \gtrless C^w = n_D\left[z - w_D^2 + w_D c^*\right] = n_D w_A c^*$$

or

$$C^u \gtreqless C^w \Leftrightarrow \frac{w_A - w_D}{w_A} \gtreqless n_D \Leftrightarrow n_A w_A \gtreqless w_D.$$

This inequality says that workfare will be preferred (less costly) to a universal transfer when the wage gap is relatively high and when the relative number of skilled workers is high. This is intuitive. Universal transfers would be expensive with a large number of skilled workers, and with a wide wage gap, the skilled workers have little temptation to waste their time in workfare.

6 Conclusion

It is now time to wrap up the main ideas of this Element. We view social protection as a public institution aimed at reducing poverty and income inequality and providing protection to all against the main risks of a lifetime. Yet the state is not the only institution doing that. The market and the family can also do it, but with their own limitations. The market does not redistribute, and the family lacks universality. Social protection is not restricted to spending; it also operates through laws and regulations that affect market and family decisions (minimum wages, parental duties). It is important to be able to assess the performance of social protection and to compare it across countries and over time. This is a difficult but feasible task. One of the big concerns of policy designers is the political sustainability of social programs, since lack of political support may lead to their slow erosion. In our democratic setting, making sure that a majority of citizens benefit from those programs is crucial. A main obstacle to performing social programs is the informational advantage that individuals have on the state or the insurance sector. Asymmetric information often leads to suboptimal policies. Reducing it even partially would be socially desirable. It matters very much to realize that the setting in which a number of social protection programs now operate is different from what it was decades ago, when they were initiated. We now face an array of social divides that our social protection must urgently address. Less emphasis on redistribution and more on social mobility might be desirable. At the close of this Element, it must be recognized that several issues have not been addressed, partly because they are new or there is not yet a consensus on how to deal with them. This is the case of the breakdown of the social elevator discussed in Section 1, which represents a real challenge for our welfare states. This is also the case with genetic tests that have the capability of improving and lengthening human life, but raise a number of legal and ethical issues. Another topic not treated, and for which there now exists some theoretical work, is long-term care for the elderly involving the market, the state, and the family. For space reasons, there is also a topic that was not dealt with, namely the matter of unemployment, particularly when it concerns the younger and the older segments of the population. This topic in itself would deserve its own Element.

Appendix

A.1 The Free Lunch in the OLG Model

The OLG Model

The basic OLG model has the following characteristics: Individuals live for two periods; in the first period of life, they are referred to as the Young. In the second period of life, they are referred to as the Old. The size of a generation t, which is also the number of young people in period t, is denoted N_t with $N_t = N_{t-1}(1 + n)$, where n denotes the rate of growth of population and $1 + n$ the number of children. People do not die early, so that the total number of the population is $P_t = N_t + N_{t-1} = N_{t-1}(2 + n)$. In the "pure exchange economy" version of the model, there is only one physical good and it cannot endure for more than one period. Each individual receives a fixed endowment of this good at birth. This endowment is denoted as w. In the "production economy" version of the model, the physical good can be either consumed or invested to build physical capital. Output is produced from labor and physical capital. Each household is endowed with one unit of time, which is inelastically supplied on the labor market.

Preferences over consumption streams are given by

$$U(c_t, d_t) = u(c_t) + \beta u(d_t),$$

where β is the rate of time preference, $u(.)$ is a strictly concave function, and c, d are the first- and the second-period consumption of the members of generation t.

From Autarky to PAYGO to Fully Funding

Consider an overlapping generation model in which identical individuals live for two periods. They have an initial endowment of w, and the rate of growth of population is $1 + n = 2$. In a world of autarky and with an unstorable good, the consumer's consumption vector is $(c, d) = (1, 0)$. We assume a log utility without time preference:

$$U_t = \log c_t + \log d_t,$$

which implies that $U_0 = -\infty$. Generation 0 has to consume its whole endowment in the first period and its second-period consumption is nil. Generation 1 expects the same scenario. It consumes w in the first period. Assume, however, that in period 2 the two generations alive, 1 and 2, adopt a social compact such that the young give to the old one-half unit of endowment with the promise that each young in the next period will give in return one-half unit of his endowment to each old. As a consequence, the old in period 2 will

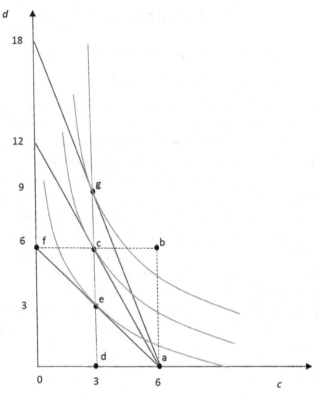

Figure 7 Free lunch and PAYGO

receive w units without having contributed to the scheme. The consumption vector of generation 1 will thus be $(c_1, d_1) = (w, w)$ and that of generation 2, $(c_2, d_2) = (1/2w, w)$. The consumption vector of generation 3 will be the same: $(c_3, d_3) = (1/2w, w)$. This can go on, but suddenly in period 5, the young decide not to give away $1/2w$ to the old of generation 4, but to invest it in a pension fund with gross return $R = 3$. This implies a consumption vector $(c_4, d_4) = (w/2, 0)$ for generation 4 and $(c_5, d_5) = (w/2, 3w/2)$ for generation 5. Those different outcomes are presented in Table 5. It appears clearly that generation 1 benefits from a free lunch, but this lunch will have to be repaid by generation 4. Those sequential solutions are depicted in Figure 7 with $w = 6$.

A Temporary Decline in Fertility

Another possible narrative is that instead of moving suddenly from a PAYGO system to a fully funded system in period 5, the PAYGO system would remain, but in period 5, the rate of growth of population would fall from 1 to 0. In that case, generation 4 would only receive a pension equal to $w/2$. As soon as the

Table 5 From PAYGO to a fully funded system

Generations/periods	U_t	c_t	d_t	
0	$-\infty$	w	0	a
1	$2\log w$	w	w	b
2	$2\log w - \log 2$	$w/2$	w	c
3	$2\log w - \log 2$	$w/2$	w	c
4	$-\infty$	$w/2$	0	d
5	$2\log w + \log 3/2$	$w/2$	$\frac{3w}{2}$	g
6	$2\log w + \log 3/2$	$w/2$	$\frac{3w}{2}$	g

Table 6 The implication of a drop in fertility with a defined contribution PAYGO

Generations/periods	U_t	c_t	d_t	
0	$-\infty$	w	0	a
1	$2\log w$	w	w	b
2	$2\log w - \log 2$	$w/2$	w	c
3	$2\log w - \log 2$	$w/2$	w	c
4	$2\log w - 2\log 2$	$w/2$	$w/2$	e
5	$2\log w - \log 2$	$w/2$	w	c
6	$2\log w - \log 2$	$w/2$	w	c

Table 7 The implication of a drop in fertility with a defined benefit PAYGO

Generations/periods	U_t	c_t	d_t	
0	$-\infty$	w	0	a
1	$2\log w$	w	w	b
2	$2\log w - \log 2$	$w/2$	w	c
3	$2\log w - \log 2$	$w/2$	w	c
4	$2\log w - \log 2$	$w/2$	w	c
5	$-\infty$	0	w	f
6	$2\log w - \log 2$	$w/2$	w	c

fertility rate goes back to $n = 1$ one period later, we go back to the consumption vector $(w/2, w)$ and so on. This is depicted in Table 6. The last column of Table 6 provides the solutions that are presented in Figure 7.

In Table 7, we keep the same demographic evolution but with a defined benefit rule. In that case the burden of the decline in fertility will fall on the young that will be forced to spend down all their endowment to keep the pension of the old at the promised level.

A.2 OLG Model with Endogenous Labor Supply and Pensions

In this section, we present an example of an OLG economy in which the age of retirement is endogenous and there is a defined benefit pension.

Consumers

We now analyze the effect of aging when the labor supply and the age of retirement are endogenous. An individual belonging to generation t lives two periods. In the first one that lasts 1, he works with an inelastic supply of labor and earns a wage w_t that is going to be used for present consumption c_t and saving s_t. In the second period, he works for a fraction of time $z_t \leq 1$ such that $1 + z_t$ can be considered as the age of retirement. Retiring early carries the utility denoted $v(1 - z)$. He will then consume d_t that is financed by the return of saving $s_t R_{t+1}$ and the second period earning $w_{t+1}z_t$. The lifetime utility of an individual belonging to generation t can be written as

$$U_t = u(c_t) + \beta [u(d_t) + v(1 - z_t)].$$

We then introduce a social security scheme such that the retirees get a fixed pension benefit $\bar{P}$, which is financed by a payroll tax paid by the young generation of workers. The rate of taxation is τ_t. The older workers do not pay the tax. This implies a revenue constraint:

$$\bar{P} = \tau_{t+1}(1 + n)w_{t+1}.$$

This PAYGO social security system has the property that it does not interfere with the retirement decision. The problem for the consumer amounts to maximizing the following lifetime utility:

$$U_t = u(w_t(1 - \tau_t) - s_t) + \beta \left[u \left(w_{t+1}z_t + s_t R_{t+1} + \bar{P} \right) + v(1 - z_t) \right],$$

where $u(.)$ and $v(.)$ are strictly concave functions and β is the time preference factor. The FOCs with respect to s and z are

$$u'(c_t) = \beta R_{t+1} u'(d_t),$$
$$v'(z_t) = u'(d_t)w_{t+1}.$$

Let us now use a log-linear specification such that the lifetime utility is

$$U_t = log(w_t(1-\tau_t)-s_t)+\beta [log (w_{t+1}[z_t + \tau_{t+1}(1+n)] + s_t R_{t+1}) + \lambda log(1-z_t]),$$

where the parameter λ denotes the preference for leisure. The FOCs are

$$\frac{\partial U_t}{\partial s_t} = -\frac{1}{w_t(1-\tau_t)-s_t} + \frac{\beta R_{t+1}}{w_{t+1}(z_t+(1+n)\tau_{t+1})+s_t R_{t+1}} = 0 \tag{5}$$

$$\frac{\partial U_t}{\partial z_t} = -\frac{w_{t+1}}{w_{t+1}(z_t+(1+n)\tau_{t+1})+s_t R_{t+1}} - \frac{\lambda}{1-z_t} \leq 0\,(=0) \Rightarrow z_t = 0\,(>0). \tag{6}$$

Depending on the parameters of the model and particularly on the preference for leisure, z_{t+1} can be nil or positive. Naturally, it cannot exceed 1.

Production

Turning to the production side, we assume a simple CRS technology such that aggregate output depends on the capital stock and the labor force. The labor force is now different from the population size as

$$L_t = N_t + N_{t-1}z_{t-1} = N_{t-1}(1+n+z_{t-1}).$$

In intensive form, we have $k = K/L$, $Y/L = y$, and

$$y_t = F(k_t, 1),$$
$$R_t = F_K(k_t, 1);\, w_t = F_L(k_t, 1).$$

With a Cobb–Douglas $y_t = k_t^\alpha$, we have

$$w_t = (1-\alpha)k_t^\alpha;\, R_t = \alpha k_t^{1-\alpha}.$$

Implicitly, we assume total depreciation of capital over the length of the generation.

Market Equilibrium

Equality between the demand and the supply of factors yields

$$K_{t+1} = N_t s_t;\, L_t = N_{t-1}(1+n+z_{t-1}).$$

We can also write

$$k_{t+1}(1+n+z_{t-1}) = s_t \tag{7}$$

and

$$R_t = R(k_t)\,;\, w_t = w(k_t).$$

Using (5) and (6), we obtain

$$z_t = \frac{1-\alpha-\alpha\lambda(1+n)-\tau_{t+1}(1-\alpha)\lambda(1+n)}{1-\lambda\alpha+\lambda}$$

and

$$k_{t+1}\left[(1+\beta)\alpha(1+n) + \tau_{t+1}(1-\alpha)(1+n)(1-\alpha) + z_t\alpha(1+\beta) + (1-\alpha)\right]$$
$$= k_t^\alpha \alpha\beta(1-\alpha)(1-\tau_t).$$

From these conditions, we can express the steady-state values of both z and k:

$$z^*(\tau) = \frac{1 - \alpha - \alpha\lambda(1+n) - \tau(1-\alpha)\lambda(1+n)}{1 - \lambda\alpha + \lambda}$$

and

$$k^*(\tau) = \left[\frac{(1-\alpha)(1-\tau)\alpha\beta}{(1+\beta)\alpha(1+n) + (1+\alpha\beta)z^*(\tau) + \tau(1-\alpha)(1+n)}\right]^{\frac{1}{1-\alpha}}.$$

If λ, the preference for leisure, is high enough, $z = 0$. In that case, we have

$$k_{z=0}^*(\tau) = \left[\frac{(1-\alpha)(1-\tau)\beta}{(1+\beta\pi)(1+n) + \frac{\tau(1-\alpha)}{\alpha}}\right]^{\frac{1}{1-\alpha}}.$$

Finally, if $\tau = 0$, we have the standard result due to Diamond (1965):

$$k_{\tau=z=0}^*(\tau) = \left[\frac{(1-\alpha)\beta}{(1+\beta\pi)(1+n)}\right]^{\frac{1}{1-\alpha}}.$$

When $z = 0$, social security clearly depresses the capital stock. When $z > 0$, this is generally not as clear, as the pension depresses z, which in turn increases k^*. This is Feldstein's induced retirement effect,[31] according to which PAYGO social security prompts earlier retirement and therefore increases the amount of retirement consumption to be financed. Empirically, it is generally accepted that a PAYGO pension depresses capital accumulation.[32]

Long-Term Social Welfare

The social planner maximizes the steady-state lifetime utility with respect to c, d, z, and k. Namely

$$U = u(f(k))\frac{1+n+z}{1+n} - \frac{d}{1+n} - (1+n+z)k) + \beta[u(d_t) + v(1-z_t)].$$

The FOCs are

$$u'(c) = \beta(1+n)u'(d); f'(k) = 1+n; \beta(v'z) = \frac{u'(c)}{i+n}[f(k) - f'(k)k]$$

or

$$R = 1+n; u'(c) = u'(d)(1+n); v'(z) = u'(d)w.$$

---

[31] Feldstein (1974).
[32] Feldstein (1974), Bosworth and Burtless (2004).

We see that the market choices of c, d, and z are optimal. The market level of k is likely to be below the Golden Rule level, particularly with a PAYGO pension system. As we have seen, the pension system discourages capital accumulation and takes us further away from the Golden Rule. This leads to an odd policy recommendation: to decentralize this optimum, one needs a negative payroll tax, implying a negative pension.

References

Adema, W. (2001). Net social expenditure, second edition, *Labor Market and Social Policy, Occasional Papers* No. 39, OECD, Paris.

Adema, W., P. Fron, and M. Ladaique (2011). Is the European welfare state really more expensive? Indicators on social spending, 1980–2012; and a manual to the OECD Social Expenditure Database (SOCX), *OECD Social, Employment and Migration Working Papers*, No. 124, OECD, Paris.

Akerlof, G. (1978). Tagging as applied to the optimal income tax, welfare programs, and manpower planning, *The American Economic* Review, 68, 8–19.

Arrow, K. (1963). Uncertainty and the welfare economics of medical care, *American Economic Review*, 53, 941–973.

Atkinson, A. B. (1991). Social insurance, *The Geneva Papers on Risk and Insurance Theory*, 16, 113–132.

Barr, N. (2020). *The Economics of the Welfare State* (6th ed.), Oxford University Press, Oxford.

Besley, T. and S. Coate (1992). Workfare versus welfare: incentive arguments for work requirement in poverty alleviation programs, *American Economic Review*, 82(1), 249–261.

Biggs, A., M. Sarney, and C. Tamborini (2009). A Progressivity Index for Social Security, Social Security Office of Retirement and Disability Policy, Issue Paper No. 2009-01, www.ssa.gov/policy/docs/issuepapers/ip2009-01.html.

Blackorby, C. and D. Donaldson (1988). Cash versus kind, self-selection and efficient transfers, *American Economics Review*, 78, 691–700.

Boadway, R., M. Marchand, M. Leite Monteiro, and P. Pestieau (2003). Social insurance and redistribution, in S. Cnossen and H.-W. Sinn (eds.), *Public Finance and Public Policy in the New Century*, Massachusetts Institute of Technology Press, Cambridge, MA, 333–358.

Bosworth, B. and G. Burtless (2004). Pension reform and saving, *National Tax Journal*, 57, 703–728.

Casamatta, G., H. Cremer, and P. Pestieau (2000). Political sustainability and the design of social insurance, *Journal of Public Economics*, 75(3), 341–364.

Cherchye, L., K. De Witte, E. Ooghe, and I. Nicaise (2010). Efficiency and equity in private and public education: a nonparametric comparison, *European Journal of Operational Research*, 202(2), 563–573.

Coelli, T. J., M. Lefebvre, and P. Pestieau (2010). On the convergence of social protection performance in the European Union, *CESIfo Economic Studies*, 56(2), 300–322.

Conde-Ruiz, I. and P. Profeta (2007). The redistributive design of social security systems, *The Economic Journal*, 117, 686–712.

Cremer, H. and F. Gahvari (1997). In-kind transfers, self-selection and optimal tax policy, *European Economic Review*, 41, 97–114.

Cremer, H. and P. Pestieau (1996). Redistributive taxation and social insurance, *International Taxation and Public Finance*, 3, 259–280.

Deleeck, H. (1979). L'effet Matthieu, *Droit Social*, 11, 375–384.

Drèze, J. and E. Schokkaert (2013). Arrow's theorem of the deductible: moral hazard and stop-loss in health insurance, *Journal of Risk and Uncertainty*, 47, 147–163.

Einav, L. and A. Finkelstein (2018). Moral hasard in health insurance: what we know and how we know it, *Journal of the European Economic Association*, 16, 957–982.

Esping-Andersen, G. (1990). *The Three Worlds of Welfare Capitalism, Princeton University Press*, Princeton.

Gruber, J. and D. Wise (1999). *Social Security and Tax on Work around the World*, NBER Book Series, The University of Chicago Press, Chicago.

Korpi, W. and J. Palme (1998). The paradox of redistribution and strategies of equality: welfare institutions, inequality, and poverty in the Western countries, *American Sociological Review*, 63(5), 661–687.

Korpi, W. and J. Palme (2003). New politics and class politics in the context of austerity and globalization: welfare states regress in 18 countries, 1975–95, *American Political Science Review*, 97, 425–446.

Lefebvre, M., S. Perelman, and P. Pestieau (2017). Productivity and performance in the public sector, in E. Grifell-Tatjé, C. A. K. Lovell, and R. C. Sickles, (eds.), *The Oxford Handbook of Productivity Analysis*, Oxford University Press, Oxford.

Merton, R. (1968). The Matthew effect in science, *Science*, 159, 56–63.

Musgrave, R. (1981). Reappraisal of financing social security. In Musgrave, R. (1986): *Public Finance in a Democratic Society*. Vol. II: Fiscal Doctrine, Growth and Institutions. New York: New York University Press, pp. 103–122.

OECD (2018). *A Broken Social Elevator? How to Promote Social Mobility*, OECD, Paris.

OECD (2020a). Social expenditure database, OECD, Paris.

OECD (2020b). Insurance indicators database, OECD, Paris.

Paulus, A., H. Sutherland, and P. Tsaklogou (2010). The distributional impact of in-kind public benefits in European countries, *Journal of Policy Analysis and Management*, 29(2), 243–266.

Pestieau, P. and M. Lefebvre (2018). *The Welfare State in Europe: Economic and Social Perspectives*, Oxford University Press, Oxford.

Rothschild, M. and J. Stiglitz (1976). Equilibrium in competitive insurance markets: an essay on the economics of imperfect information, *Quarterly Journal of Economics*, 90, 629–649.

Rochet, J.-Ch. (1991). Incentives, redistribution and social insurance, *The Geneva Papers on Risk and Insurance Theory*, 16, 143–166.

Sorensen, P.-B. (2003). Social insurance based on individual savings accounts, in S. Cnossen and H.-W. Sinn, eds., *Public Finance in the New Millennium*, Massachusetts Institute of Technology Press.

Yaari, M. (1965). Uncertain lifetime, life Insurance, and the theory of the consumer. *Review of Economic Studies*, 32(2), 137–150.

Acknowledgments

Support from the the TSE-SCOR "Risk Markets and Value Creation" Chair is acknowledged. I am also grateful to Jerome Schoenmakers for the tables and the figures and to one of the editors and two referees for insightful comments.

Cambridge Elements

Public Economics

Robin Boadway
Queen's University

Robin Boadway is Emeritus Professor of Economics at Queen's University. His main research interests are in public economics, welfare economics and fiscal federalism.

Frank A. Cowell
London School of Economics and Political Science

Frank A. Cowell is Professor of Economics at the London School of Economics. His main research interests are in inequality, mobility and the distribution of income and wealth.

Massimo Florio
University of Milan

Massimo Florio is Professor of Public Economics at the University of Milan. His main interests are in cost-benefit analysis, regional policy, privatization, public enterprise, network industries and the socio-economic impact of research infrastructures.

About the Series

The Cambridge Elements of Public Economics provides authoritative and up-to-date reviews of core topics and recent developments in the field. It includes state-of-the-art contributions on all areas in the field. The editors are particularly interested in the new frontiers of quantitative methods in public economics, experimental approaches, behavioral public finance, empirical and theoretical analysis of the quality of government and institutions.

Cambridge Elements $\equiv$

Public Economics

Elements in the Series

A full series listing is available at: www.cambridge.org/ElePubEcon

Printed in the United States
by Baker & Taylor Publisher Services